Aytek Çingitaş

Violations of human rights to justify intervention on the basis of the responsibility to protect (R2P)

GRIN Publishing

Bibliographic information published by the German National Library:

The German National Library lists this publication in the National Bibliography; detailed bibliographic data are available on the Internet at http://dnb.dnb.de .

Imprint:

Copyright © 2014 GRIN Verlag GmbH
Print and binding: Books on Demand GmbH, Norderstedt Germany
ISBN: 978-3-656-86873-6

This book at GRIN:

http://www.grin.com/en/e-book/286512/violations-of-human-rights-to-justify-intervention-on-the-basis-of-the

GRIN - Your knowledge has value

Since its foundation in 1998, GRIN has specialized in publishing academic texts by students, college teachers and other academics as e-book and printed book. The website www.grin.com is an ideal platform for presenting term papers, final papers, scientific essays, dissertations and specialist books.

Visit us on the internet:

http://www.grin.com/

http://www.facebook.com/grincom

http://www.twitter.com/grin_com

Content

Introduction

In this paper, I will try to find an answer to the question; *"Do violations of human rights justify intervention on the basis of the responsibility to protect? In what cases?"* with a specific focus on NATO intervention to Kosovo that took place in 1999. In the first part of the paper, I will analyze the history, development, principles and background of Responsibility Protect principle (R2P in short) in a summary. In the second part of the paper, I will show the reader at which cases (when) this principle may be justified by human rights violations. In this part, I will mainly analyze which level of human rights violations should be present in order to justify a military intervention as a part of R2P. In the third part of the paper, I will study on 1999 NATO intervention to Kosovo as a case study and I will try to find an answer to the question; *"Was 1999 NATO intervention to Kosovo an example of R2P?"*

History, Background and Principles of R2P in a Summary

Until 1990's, majority of international relations scholars, state policies and international organizations policies were dominated by state centric approach, which opposites to any interventions to the states and considers the state sovereignty as the key element of international relations.[1] State centric approach, which is based on state sovereignty, naturally is also formed on the idea of nonintervention. The ideas of nonintervention and importance of state sovereignty were historically developed from Westphalia Treaty of 1648 and became an international consensus and agreement between the states.[2] The ideas of nonintervention and untouchable state sovereignty were also reinforced later by Montevideo Convention (1933), League of Nations Covenant (1920) and Charter of UN (1945).[3] So it can be said that, historically, states have always kept their right to control their domestic politics without interferences by other states or any external powers.[4]

However, as a result of the massive human rights violations and civilian killings in

---

[1] *Evans, 2008, p. 16.*
[2] *Janzekovic, 2013, p. 14.*
[3] *Ibidem.*
[4] *Janzekovic, 2013, p. 16.*

1990's, international community started to debate what sovereignty actually means and what should be done if a sovereign state fails to protect its citizens or massively violates the human rights of their citizens. [5] After the humanity faced the dramatic massacres – especially in Bosnia and Rwanda- in 1990's, ideas intending to justify interventions in order to protect civilians and human rights started to be spoken. In this context, international community, world powers and international organizations (especially UN) aimed to form a new principle that can legally justify the interventionist idea for humanitarian aims. [6] This idea started to get considered and debated loudly in international arena in the late 1990's in order not to have more Rwandas or Kosovos. [7]

With these triggers, in September 2000; the Canadian Government announced at UN General Assembly that they launched the "International Commission on Intervention and State Sovereignty" (ICISS). Main goal of ICISS was to promote the idea of humanitarian intervention as a responsibility for international community and to find an international consensus on dealing with the states that are failing to protect its citizens in crisis situations. ICISS tried to find a balancing solution on the ongoing debate between the value of humanitarian intervention and the value of state sovereignty. [8] ICISS published its first and only report, entitled "The Responsibility to Protect" in December 2001. This report briefly cited that; *"Where a population is suffering serious harm, as a result of internal war, insurgency, repression or state failure, and the state in question is unwilling or unable to halt or avert it, the principle of non-intervention yields to the international responsibility to protect."*[9]

With the release of its only report, ICISS completed its mandate. Although it was not fully implemented by all states at that time, the R2P principle has had some success in getting into the international agenda by the efforts of ICISS. State officials, UN and NGO's started to use the language of "responsibility to protect" in relation to serious

[5] *Bellamy, 2010, p. 270-272.*
[6] *Ibidem, p. 270-272.*
[7] *Morris, 2013, p. 1269.*
[8] *Janzekovic, 2013, p. 45.*
[9] *ICISS Report, 2001, p. XI.*

humanitarian crises and military interventions as a response to them. [10]

Then, the biggest step for international acceptance of R2P was the outcome of UN Sixtieth Anniversary World Summit in September 2005.[11] The UN's unanimous adoption and approval of R2P as part of its 2005 World Summit outcome document meant that each UN member state accepted R2P as a principle under the scope and limits of outcome document.

In paragraph 138 of the outcome document, all UN members accepted that; *'each individual State has the responsibility to protect its populations from genocide, war crimes, ethnic cleansing and crimes against humanity';* and in paragraph 139 it is accepted that; *'the international community, through the United Nations ... is prepared to take collective action, in a timely and decisive manner, through the Security Council, in accordance with the Charter, including Chapter VII'* to protect populations from those acts.[12]

After the international acceptance of R2P, we can see that the dominant idea of "state centric approach" in international relations has been replaced by "interventionist approach". Frankly, nowadays it is hard to find an international law or international relations expert / scholar who completely supports state centric approach.[13] Also, with R2P, international community had found the legalized way to protect citizens of failing states and intervene to those states in crisis situations. One may also think that, with R2P principle, powerful states have found the "legalized" way to intervene to certain areas of world towards their geographical, strategic or resource based interests. [14]

It can also be said that, after the R2P principle, the understanding of humanitarian intervention as a *"right"* of the states to intervene to other states changed into a *"responsibility"* of the states to protect other (failed) states' citizens. [15] In my opinion,

---

[10] *Pattison, 2010, p. 3.*
[11] *Evans, 2008, p. 44.*
[12] *UN World Summit Outcome Document, 2005.*
[13] *Pattison, 2010 p. 2.*
[14] *Brown, 2010, p. 313-314*
[15] *Brown, 2010, p. 18-19.*

different usage of the words "right" and "responsibility" is an effort of the powerful states to justify their military interventions to other states and to gain sympathy in the eyes of public opinion. [16]

ICISS was aware that the key factor to succeed in promoting the interventionist idea was to find a balance between protection of human rights and the failed state's sovereignty.[17] Because of this, ICISS carefully cited the principles and requirements of military intervention and marked the military intervention as a *"last resort"* for R2P.[18] The *"last resort"* principle is also followed by the UN in 2005 World Summit outcome document, which will be analyzed in the second part of this paper.

At this juncture, I must stress that military intervention is not equal to R2P but it is a part of R2P. Mainly, R2P principle is formed of three main pillars (responsibilities) which are; "The responsibility to prevent", "The responsibility to react" and "The responsibility to rebuild". Military intervention is just a part of the "responsibility to react", which may be practiced only in extreme cases as a last resort. [19] Nevertheless, unfortunately we see that R2P principle is merely understood as a justifying principle for *military interventions* to the failing states. Even the head of states usually cannot distinguish these two concepts, as their policies are usually towards a *"do nothing or send the soldiers"* approach as Lee Feinstein mentions.[20] Being very well aware of the difference between R2P and military intervention, I will principally focus on military interventions as a part of R2P in the following parts.

If we turn back to ICISS's efforts on the topic, we see that ICISS tried to remark the limits and conditions[21] of military intervention, but did the international community manage to comply with these limits and conditions in the interventions practiced so far? Or did they act as military intervention is the first resort and only solution for R2P and

---

[16] *Janzekovic, 2013, p. 73-74.*
[17] *Orford, 2013, p. 101.*
[18] *ICISS Report, 2001, p. XII.*
[19] *ICISS Report, 2001, p. XI.*
[20] *Feinstein, 2007, p. 48.*
[21] *ICISS Report, 2001, p. XII-XIII.*

always '*sent the marines instead of doing nothing?*'[22]

As a conclusion for the first part, we can say that the R2P principle (in form of military interventions in extraordinary cases) as a response to the mass violation of basic human rights are universally accepted between the sovereign states, international organizations and international community. In short, it is universally accepted that massive human rights violations may justify the interventions on the basis of R2P. But the clash of ideas between the states and the international community emerges with this question; *"When and in which conditions the human rights violations may justify military interventions?"*

By Which Human Rights Violations and When are the Military Interventions (as a part of R2P) Justified?

Frankly, it is very difficult to keep crimes against humanity as a secret in this age of technological improvements and global communications.[23] So, it can easily be said that international community is well aware of what is going on and which human rights are being violated in any part of the global world. Thereafter, the main question arises; when are military interventions justified (by which) Human Rights Violations?

The very first answer to this question can be found in ICISS report, which cites that '*there must be serious and irreparable harm occurring to human beings, or imminently likely to occur, of the following kind to start a military intervention;*

large scale loss of life, actual or apprehended, with genocidal intent or not, which is the product either of deliberate state action, or state neglect or inability to act, or a failed state situation; or large scale 'ethnic cleansing', actual or apprehended, whether carried out by killing, forced expulsion, acts of terror or rape.'[24]

If we answer the question from the UN point of view, which is based on 2005 World

---

[22] *Feinstein, 2007, p. 48.*
[23] *Janzekovic, 2006, p. 74.*
[24] *ICISS Report, 2001, p. XII.*

Summit outcome document, our answer slightly differs. According to paragraph 138 of the outcome document, the entire UN membership accepts that; *'each individual State has the responsibility to protect its populations from genocide, war crimes, ethnic cleansing and crimes against humanity';* and paragraph 139 declares that *'the international community, through the United Nations ... is prepared to take collective action, in a timely and decisive manner, through the Security Council, in accordance with the Charter, including Chapter VII'* to protect populations from the four mentioned acts.[25]

So, according to the paragraph 138 of outcome document, military interventions can be justified only in more limited situations than the ICISS report, which are *'genocide, war crimes, ethnic cleansing and crimes against humanity'* whereas according to ICISS report, large scale loss of life (with genocidal intent or not) is even sufficient.

We see that, both in ICISS report and world summit outcome document, R2P situations are the mass atrocity crimes involving genocide, ethnic cleansing or other war crimes or crimes against humanity which are occurring or about to occur or where the situation could get worse if necessary measures are not taken.[26] As made clear by ICISS report and outcome document, military intervention for humanitarian purposes is an extremely serious, extraordinary and exceptional matter.[27] By this, we see that military intervention is a 'last resort' according to UN policy as well as ICISS doctrine.[28]

Besides the similarities and slight differences between ICISS doctrine and the World Summit doctrine that mentioned above, there are also some important differences between their understandings of R2P while answering the question of *'When to intervene?'*[29] These main differences are as;

1- In the ICISS doctrine of R2P; International community has the responsibility to

[25] *UN World summit outcome document, 2005, p. 30.*
[26] *Evans, 2008, p. 226.*
[27] *Ibidem, p. 59.*
[28] *Ibidem, p. 57.*
[29] *Pattison, 2010, p. 14.*

protect when the failing state is *unable* or *unwilling* to protect its citizens' human rights. [30] Whereas according to UN policy, international community has the responsibility to protect only when *'national authorities are manifestly failing to protect their populations'*.[31]

2- In ICISS doctrine, when the state fails to act, international community has a *fallback* responsibility. [32] In UN doctrine, international community does not have a fallback responsibility to react to the crisis. Rather, international community (states) is only *'prepared'* to take collective action *'on a case-by-case basis'*.[33]

3- According to ICISS report, the Security Council is the first authority to authorize an intervention, but alternative authorities are also possible. [34] According to UN doctrine, the act of intervention must be collective and Security Council is the *only* authority to authorize the intervention. [35]

4- According to ICISS report, intervention must also meet four additional principles such as right intention, last resort, proportional means, and reasonable prospects. [36] Right intention means the primary motivation or purpose of the military action (whether if it is mainly to stop the threat, or has another main objective); last resort means whether there are any other possible peaceful (unarmed) alternatives to solve the crisis, the proportionality of the response means the intervention should be proportionate to the ongoing crisis; and the balance of consequences which can also be mentioned as *"no harm rule"*, which means more good than harm should be done by the intervention.[37] But in UN doctrine, there are no principles for intervention such as the four principles mentioned in the ICISS report.

In my opinion, and also as Evans mentions; [38] apart from the above-mentioned

---

[30] *ICISS Report, 2001, p. 17.*
[31] *UN World summit outcome document, 2005, p. 30.*
[32] *ICISS Report, 2001, p. 17.*
[33] *UN World summit outcome document, 2005, p. 30.*
[34] *ICISS Report, 2001, p. 53.*
[35] *UN World summit outcome document, 2005, p. 30.*
[36] *ICISS Report, 2001, p. XII.*
[37] *Evans, 2008, p. 60.*
[38] *Evans, 2008, p.74.*

principles, one of the most important other principle or fact to take into account while answering the *'When to intervene?'* question is the failing state's history. However, this fact has not been mentioned in ICISS report or World Summit outcome document because of the fragile relations between the states and international community.

If the failing state has a history of mass killings committed by its past governments or by different ethnic, social or religious groups in the country against other groups, these countries should be watched carefully and any small spark of a humanitarian crisis ongoing in these countries should be urgently taken into consideration by the international community. As Evans mentions; *'One of the best single indicators of future conflict is past conflict, and unhappily the same seems to hold true for atrocity crimes.'* [39]

Also as Janzekovic [40] and Evans [41] mentions; 1999 NATO intervention to Kosovo can easily be a good an example of Evans's above-mentioned phrase. Before this intervention, international community was very well aware of Yugoslav and Serbian authorities' intolerable histories on mass killings, especially occurred in 1992 Bosnian war. Because of this awareness, international community –formed as NATO in this case- acted very quickly although there was not a UN Security Council resolution for the intervention. The international community has seen the risk because of Serbia's (Yugoslavia's) history and took the first tiny spark into consideration. Though, 1999 Kosovo intervention is criticized by many scholars and experts who cites that international community acted too much and too soon in this intervention.

As a conclusion for this part; we see that both in ICISS doctrine and in UN policy of R2P, mass atrocity crimes involving genocide, ethnic cleansing or other war crimes or crimes against humanity –of course provided with the principles mentioned- are sufficient human rights violations that are justifying military interventions.

---

[39] *Evans, 2008, p. 74.*
[40] *Janzekovic, 2013, p. 5-6.*
[41] *Evans, 2008, p. 29.*

Was 1999 NATO intervention to Kosovo an example of R2P?

It can easily be said that, Kosovo intervention is one of the most debated military interventions throughout the history of interventionist idea. As I mentioned in the second part, international community was very alert on the Kosovo conflict because of the past mass killings committed by the same authorities and groups in the same geographical region. [42] So, when the Serb military started to commit human rights violations against Albanian civilians in 1998, United States of America and its allies (formed as NATO in this case) took immediate action and started an air campaign against Serbia (Yugoslavia) although there was not a Security Council resolution authorizing the intervention. Though, NATO's intervention was successful at preventing the violations and didn't let them get massive as experienced in Bosnian war. International community also supported the intervention; even the Independent International Commission on Kosovo cited that the intervention was *'legitimate, but not legal under existing international law* [43]. This situation led Kosovo intervention to be mentioned as *"illegal but legitimate"* which also means that, the Kosovo intervention didn't fulfill the 'right authority' principle. [44]

Another principle the international community failed to fulfill in Kosovo intervention was 'balance of consequences' (no harm) principle. In Kosovo intervention, NATO bombed the Serb positions from high altitude, rather than exposing their military aircraft to Serbian radars or anti-aircraft fires. NATO did not also use ground troops at the beginning of the intervention, which would lead to casualties and a decrease in the support to the operation from its members. Many of the civilian casualties were because of NATO air attacks and its engagement rules dictated that NATO military aircraft must fly higher than 10.000 feet during the air campaign, which made aircrafts safe from Serbian radars and fire. As a result of this air attack practiced by NATO, more civilians were killed than might the ground forces would have been used.[45]

---

[42] *Evans, 2008, p. 29.*
[43] *Independent International Commission on Kosovo, Kosovo Report, 2000, p. 289.*
[44] *Brown, 2010, p. 314.*
[45] *Mills, 2013, p. 354.*

NATO's choice about high-altitude bombing increased civilian casualties on the ground. [46] After the air campaign, a settlement was reached only when NATO finally threatened the Serbian authorities about inserting the ground troops.[47]

The Kosovo intervention still continues to generate counter arguments on its merits, in particular it was illegal and that NATO caused more harm than good. But the overall opinion of international community generally agrees that the intervention was justifiable in those circumstances. So, we can see that international community is questioning the NATO intervention not about its legitimacy but rather its legality, as a result of the lack of a Security Council resolution. [48]

Though, especially with the current Syrian conflict, it is still being asked that waiting for a resolution from the Security Council in urgent crisis situations is not a good idea maybe. Unfortunately, the power [im]balance and the bloc approach (the veto powers of the permanent members) in the Security Council makes the Council functionless to take critic decisions. Because of this, the Security Council often fails to take a decision on interventions when it is really needed, as it is seen in ongoing Syrian crisis. Also in Kosovo case, NATO looked for a Security Council resolution for the intervention, but the Security Council got paralyzed because of Russian ties to the Milosevic regime.[49] I believe, the reason that Security Council is paralyzed again in these days on Syrian crisis is the same, which are Russia's ties with Assad regime and China's customary non-interventionist approach throughout the years.

On the other hand, Kosovo intervention still raises questions about the intervening state's legal status. Because, if states can intervene freely and completely outside the principles of the UN, as in Kosovo,[50] and if military interventions can be successful at stopping human rights violations without a legal authorization or basis, does the intervening state really need a legal right -a Security Council resolution- to intervene?

---

[46] Jackson, 2010, p. 319
[47] Evans, 2008, p. 29.
[48] Ibidem.
[49] Pattison, 2010, p.6.
[50] Ibidem, p. 25.

BIBLIOGRAPHY

1- Bellamy Alex J. & Reike Ruben, 'The Responsibility to Protect and International Law', pp. 267-286 in *Global Responsibility to Protect*, vol. 2, 2010.

2- Brown Chris, 'On Gareth Evans, The Responsibility to Protect: Ending Mass Atrocity Crimes Once and for All', pp. 310-314 in *Global Responsibility to Protect*, vol. 2, 2010.

3- Evans Gareth, *The Responsibility to Protect: Ending Mass Atrocity Crimes Once and For All*. Washington D.C.: The Brookings Institution, 2008.

4- Feinstein Lee, *Darfur and Beyond: What Is Needed to Prevent Mass Atrocities*. New York: Council on Foreign Relations, 2007.

5- Independent International Commission on Kosovo, *Kosovo Report*. Oxford: Oxford University Press, 2000.

6- International Commission on Intervention and State Sovereignty (ICISS), *The Responsibility to Protect: Report of the International Commission on Intervention and State Sovereignty*. Ottawa: International Development Research Centre, 2001.

7- Jackson Robert, 'War Perils in the Responsibility to Protect', pp. 315-319 in *Global Responsibility to Protect*, vol. 2, 2010.

8- Janzekovic John & Silander Daniel, *Responsibility to Protect and Prevent: Principles, Promises and Practicalities*. London: Anthem Press, 2013.

9- Janzekovic John, *The Use of Force in Humanitarian Intervention: Morality and Practicalities*. Hampshire: Ashgate Publishing, 2006.

10- Mills Kurt, 'R2P: Protecting, Prosecuting, or Palliating in Mass Atrocity Situations?', pp. 333-356 in *Journal of Human Rights*, vol. 12, 2013.

11- Morris Justin, 'Libya and Syria: R2P and the spectre of the swinging pendulum', pp. 1265-1283 in *International Affairs,* vol. 89: 5, 2013.

12- Orford Anne, 'Moral Internationalism and the Responsibility to Protect', pp. 83–108 in *The European Journal of International Law*, vol. 24, no. 1, 2013.

13- Pattison James, Humanitarian Intervention and Responsibility to Protect: Who Should Intervene? New York: Oxford University Press, 2010.

14- United Nations (UN), *2005 World Summit Outcome*. New York: United Nations, 2005.